ChemungHistory.com's

DELUXE Big Book of Pictures

By Diane Janowski

New York History Review

Elmira, New York

ChemungHistory.com's DELUXE Big Book of Pictures
by Diane Janowski
Copyright ©2009 & 2022 New York History Review. All rights reserved.

Notice of Rights. No part of this book may be reproduced or transmitted in any form by any means, mechanical, photocopying, recording or otherwise, without the prior written permission of the author. For more information on getting permission for reprints contact us through our website. NewYorkHistoryReview.com

ISBN: 978-1-950822-28-7

Second printing.
Printed in the United States of America.

Front cover. The Mark Twain Hotel, circa 1929.
Publisher: Rubin Brothers, Elmira.

Table of Contents

Street scenes..7

Buildings..32

Churches..71

City Parks...79

Rorick's Glen..95

Eldridge Park..100

Chemung River...110

Trains and Railroads..................................127

Elmira College..130

Landscapes...138

Mark Twain...149

Bibliography...157

ChemungHistory.com and New York History Review proudly present our *BIG Book of Pictures*. We are pleased to share images from our collection of postcards and photographs in the Eleanor Barnes Library in Elmira, New York.

These wonderful old images of Elmira and Chemung County are sure to heighten your interest in the rich cultural heritage of the Chemung Valley region.

Diane Janowski, Publisher
New York History Review

Opposite page: This 1854 albumen stereograph view of Lake Street looking north from Water Street is attributed to Abraham Hart. Hart's studio was around the corner on Water Street. The albumen process using egg white as applied sizing was a brand new process and Hart would have been considered "cutting edge" for his time. That animal is not a dog - it's a pig.

Street Scenes

A view of Elmira in June 1859 looking north on old State Street (today's Clemens' Center Parkway) from the *Telegram* newspaper building on Market Street. The first cross street is East Gray Street and the second, with the church steeples, is East Church Street. Publisher: Excelsior View Company, Elmira.

Opposite page: An albumen stereograph view by Elisha Van Aken of the Chemung Canal in Elmira" looking northwest from the Hose Tower" [the fire station on Market Street] circa 1870. This portion of the canal was filled in around 1873 to make State Street - see above. The bridge over the canal is today's East Gray Street.

J.E. Larkin took this albumen stereograph view of Baldwin Street looking north circa 1870. The Rathbun Hotel is on the left. Note the unattended baby in the stroller. John Edward Larkin was a pioneer in photography in Elmira. His studio opened in 1858 on Water Street and closed in the 1880s. Larkin is well known for his photographs of the Elmira Prison Camp.

Fire struck the Elmira *Advertiser* newspaper building in 1888 on the corner of Market and Lake Streets. Two employees were killed. Eventually the Mohican/Mohawk Market was built on this spot. This is an albumen print by an unknown photographer.

An albumen stereograph view by Elisha Van Aken, circa 1880. The handwritten caption reads "Elmira, looking north from the hose tower" (fire department on East Market Street). The churches are First Presbyterian on the left (razed in 1967 to make way for Elm Chevrolet), and First Methodist on the right (razed in 1965). Note all the houses.

An Elisha Van Aken albumen stereograph view of East Water Street looking west (the big building on the right is on the corner of Lake Street), circa 1880.

An albumen stereograph view of Carroll Street by J. E. Larkin looking west with the Rathbun Hotel in the distance. On the right are the offices of the Elmira *Daily* and *Weekly Gazette*. The *Daily Gazette* ran from 1860 to 1907.

An albumen print of Dewitt Avenue looking south from East Clinton Street toward East Third Street, June 1, 1889. This was the same day as the Johnstown (Pennsylvania) flood. Publisher: Excelsior View Company, Elmira.

A postcard view looking north on Lake Street from Water Street, circa 1905. Some of these buildings are still standing. Publisher: unknown.

A postcard view of East Water Street looking east from Railroad Avenue, circa 1905. Publisher: unknown.

The Elmira *Telegram* newspaper fire on March 13, 1913 destroyed four buildings on State Street from the corner of East Market Street toward East Water Street, including the Elmira *Telegram*, the Amusu Theatre, Connelly's grocery, Thompson's Wholesale, and the Knights of Columbus hotel. The fire occurred directly across the street from the fire station. Photograph courtesy of the Barnes family.

A postcard view of East Water Street looking east from Railroad Avenue, circa 1922. Note the old Chemung Canal Bank (the light-colored building in the middle). The buildings on the left are now the area of the WETM television studio. Publisher: Rubin Brothers, Elmira.

LOOKING SOUTH FROM TOWER OF VILLAGE HALL, ELMIRA HEIGHTS, N. Y.

This is a view looking south from Elmira Heights, circa 1895. The factory is the Elmira Window Glass Works between 9th and 11th Streets.

A postcard view looking west on Church Street, circa 1890. The cross street is Walnut Street. Glove House is the second on the right. Publisher: Hugh C. Leighton, Portland, ME.

William Street, on Elmira's Eastside, was once an elegant neighborhood with large homes and yards. Postcard image circa 1907. Publisher: unknown.

A view of West Water Street, circa 1929. Publisher: Ruben Publishing, Newburgh.

Looking north on Main Street from the bridge, circa 1925. Some of these buildings still exist. Publisher: Rubin Brothers, Elmira.

Lake and Water Streets looking west, circa 1932. On the left is the Hulett Building - Elmira's first "skyscraper" with 6 stories. It was razed after the 1972 flood. Note the "traffic tower" with an attendant who changed the lights. Publisher: Rubin Brothers, Elmira.

West Water Street looking east toward the newly elevated train tracks, circa 1934. Publisher: Rubin Brothers, Elmira.

The same view as on the opposite page twenty years earlier. Sheehan Dean's was new to this location in 1910. Publisher: unknown.

East Water Street looking west from Lake Street, circa 1919. Several of the buildings on the right still exist. Publisher: unknown.

EAST WATER STREET, BY MOONLIGHT, ELMIRA, N. Y.

"East Water Street by Moonlight." The same image as on the opposite page but this time it has an artistic twist. Publisher: Rub n Brothers, Elmira.

Lake and Water Streets looking west, circa 1890. The Arnot Building stood on the corner. Publisher: unknown.

West Water Street looking west, circa 1930. Publisher: Ruben Publishing, Newburgh.

Buildings

Postcard view looking east on East Church Street, circa 1900. The Post Office is on the right and the First Presbyterian Church is on the left. Publisher: Jeannette Adams, Elmira.

The Century Club organized in 1880 as a social club of prominent professional and business men. Their bylaws prohibited the consumption of alcohol and gambling. This new building was built in 1906. There were bowling alleys in the basement and daily lunches were served. The club disbanded during the Depression. This building still exists as the Yunis offices. Publisher: Rubin Brothers, Elmira.

The Arnot-Ogden Hospital on Roe Avenue was Elmira's first hospital and opened in 1888. This view is circa 1900. This old building does not exist, but many new buildings have been added. Publisher: Rochester News Company, Rochester, NY.

St. Joseph's Hospital opened on Market Street in 1907. This annex was built in 1914 on High Street and contained a medical ward on the first floor, a maternity ward on the second, and classrooms and dining room in the basement. The hospital has grown and rebuilt itself many times since. Publisher: Rubin Brothers, Elmira.

The first Steele Memorial Library opened in 1899 on the corner of Lake and Market Streets. Mrs. Esther Baker Steele donated this building as a memorial to her husband, Joel Dorman Steele. The Carnegie Corporation donated the second Steele library building on East Church Street in 1921. The third, and current, library building is also on East Church Street. This building was razed in the early 1960s. Publisher: unknown.

A postcard view of the second Steele Memorial Library donated by the Carnegie Corporation in the 1920s. The third library opened in 1979 several blocks west. Publisher: Queen City Paper Co., Elmira.

The Old City Hall, now occupied by the Alpha Club, Elmira, N. Y.

The old city hall building on Market Street was used from 1860 until 1896. Before that it was the Chemung County Courthouse. It was razed to make way for the Elks Club's new facility in 1911. Publisher: Miss Jeannette Adams.

This postcard shows a view of the 1894 portion of the Chemung County Courthouse complex on Lake Street. The buildings are a distinguished example of Gothic architecture. Gladke Park is in front of the buildings and showcases this Civil War monument. Publisher: The Buffalo News Company, Buffalo.

A view of the Chemung County Courthouse, circa 1910. Publisher: American News Company, New York.

Postcard view of the Gas Works building on Madison Avenue, circa 1910. It was built in 1848. Later it became the Elmira Water, Light and Railroad building. The EWL&R erected poles with electric lights to light streets, and electric lines to supply power to homes and businesses in Elmira. The building still stands. Publisher: unknown.

The Conewawah Inn, across from the Elmira Knitting Mill, circa 1895. This was a boarding house for the women who worked in the factory. The mill was founded in 1893 by William Bilbrough and Casper Decker and closed in 1963. The mill made military clothing during World War II. This building still stands on the corner of Prescott Avenue and East 18th Street.

The Masonic Temple, circa 1895. Note the mansard roof and cupola. The temple suffered a massive fire in 1914 and lost the top two floors. Architects redesigned the top differently. Since 1972 it is Chemung County's "Hazlett Building." Publisher: Buffalo News Company, Buffalo, NY.

Postcard view of the Mozart Theater on East Market Street, circa 1917. Not named for Wolfgang Amadeus Mozart, but rather Ed Mozart, who opened it in 1908. Eventually it became the Strand Theater and closed in 1957. The building was razed in 1967. Publisher: unknown.

ARNOT ART GALLERY, ELMIRA, N. Y.

The Arnot Art Museum was originally built as the home of John Arnot, and later his son Matthias Arnot lived there. Matthias died in 1910 and bequeathed his art collection to the public. In 1913, the building opened as the Arnot Art Gallery. It became the Arnot Art Museum in 1969. Publisher: Rubin Brothers, Elmira.

Buildings at the Elmira Civil War Prison Camp, original photograph attributed to J. E. Larkin, circa 1864. Publisher: Hugh C. Leighton Company, Portland, ME.

The Post Office building on the corner of East Church and old State Streets, built in 1903, still exists and is awaiting a revival. The lobby had Vermont marble walls, oak woodwork, and a beautiful marble staircase. Publisher: Paul C. Koeber Company, NY.

One of Chemung County's first settlers was John Hendy. Hendy had been here with General Sullivan in 1779, and liked the area so much that he returned after the war. In spring 1788, he built his first cabin near the mouth of Newtown Creek at the Chemung River. Later that year he built this cabin in the vicinity of today's Rorick's Glen Parkway and West Water Street. This dwelling no longer exists but it did survive until the early 20th century. Publisher: unknown.

The New York State Armory building on East Church Street. This building still stands at this writing, but it is awaiting its fate. Publisher: unknown.

The New York State Reformatory opened in 1876. Superintendent Zebulon Brockway believed that inmates needed more than punishment, and tried to provide them a proper education, recreation, and discipline during their time in Elmira. Note the fancy turrets on the building. Photograph courtesy of the Barnes family.

A postcard view of a dress parade inside the New York State Reformatory, circa 1910. Publisher: C. S. Woolworth Company, Elmira.

It says "Rathburn" but it should be "Rathbun." The hotel (formerly the Brainard House) was on the northwest corner of East Water and Baldwin Streets - now the area of the Chemung Canal Bank. The building was razed in 1941. Publisher: Rubin Brothers, Elmira.

5—Mark Twain Hotel, Elmira, N. Y.

The Mark Twain Hotel on West Gray Street, circa 1950. It opened in May 1929 just seven months before the stock market crash. Today it is an apartment building. Publisher: Rubin Brothers, Elmira.

The Dininny residence, built in 1872, was possibly the finest and most expensive house in Elmira. Located on the northeast corner of West Water Street and Guinnip Avenue, it was the home of Ferral Dininny who made his fortune in coal. Dininny died in 1901 and the house was torn down in 1910. Publisher: Hugh C. Leighton Company, Portland, ME.

The "Strathmont" mansion was first built in 1896 by J. Sloat Fassett on a 47-acre plot. The home had 53 rooms. It was torn down and rebuilt in 1928 by J. Arnot Rathbone. This is the first structure - the second structure still exists. Publisher: Rubin Brothers, Elmira.

The State Line Hotel on Route 14, at the Pennsylvania state line - was a stage coach stop on the toll road that connected Elmira and northern Pennsylvania. In 1852 the road was 13-feet wide and made of hemlock planks. Hotels and taverns along the way made the 6-mile trip nicer. The building still exists. Photograph by Allen C. Smith, 2008.

This is a view of the Women's Federation Building, on the corner of East Church and old State Streets, circa 1910. This building united all the community services under one roof. It was razed in the late 1970s to make way for the Steele Memorial Library. Publisher: unknown.

Elmira's City Hall on the corner of East Church and Lake Streets. Built in 1896 from designs by Elmira architects Pierce & Bickford, reminiscent of the World Columbian Exposition. The pediments are decorated with figures representing agriculture, arts, and science. The building suffered a massive fire on November 18, 1909 with heavy damage to the interior. The roof and clock tower collapsed. The clock tower was rebuilt. Publisher: Paul C. Koeber Co., New York City.

Directly across the street from City Hall is the Elmira City Club. The private club started in 1899 and eventually moved to this location. The club still exists and is used for luncheons, private dinners, and business deals. Publisher: Jeannette Adams, Elmira.

This beautiful house was the home of Mayor Daniel Sheehan. It was designed by Elmira architects Pierce & Bickford and built in 1894. The Sheehan family lived here for 31 years and then it was a boarding house/apartment house for many years. Since 1983 it has been the "Christmas House." Publisher: Rubin Brothers, Elmira.

The *Star-Gazette* newspaper building on the corner of Baldwin and Market Streets, circa 1910. Publisher: Baker Brothers, Elmira.

Town Clock. Elmira, N. Y.

The Town Clock was in the J. Richardson & Company building, circa 1890, in the area where Market Street and Railroad Avenue used to cross. Richardson made 1,600 pairs of shoes daily in the late 1800s - the business closed in 1908. The clock was made by the Seth Thomas Company, and the Reverend Thomas K. Beecher was its caretaker. The building was razed in 1962 for the Centertown parking lot. Publisher: Buffalo News Company, Buffalo.

The Elmira Knitting Mill on Prescott Avenue in Elmira Heights, circa 1900. The factory was open from 1893 to 1963. The building still exists. Publisher: unknown.

The American-LaFrance company on Erie Street on the Southside made fire engines and fire equipment. The company opened in 1903 and closed in 1985 in Elmira. The company still exists in Summerville, South Carolina. Only a few of these buildings still exist. Publisher: Rubin Brothers, Elmira.

An albumen print of the Elmira Window Glass Works on Eleventh Street near Elmwood Avenue in Elmira Heights, circa 1895. Owned by Matthias Arnot and A. M. Bennett. The business was sold and moved south in 1904. The buildings were razed in 1914. Photographer: unknown.

Postcard view of the Philo National Poultry Institute on Lake Street in Elmira. The building still exists but is not in use. Ernest Philo invented new incubators and techniques for raising strong, well-adjusted chickens and roosters. Chicken people came from all over the US to attend classes and purchase equipment. Mr. Philo closed the Institute before 1919. Publisher: Rubin Brothers, Elmira.

The George M. Diven School on Hall Street, circa 1940. Building still in use. Publisher: Rubin Brothers, Elmira.

This is the second of three Elmira Free Academy buildings on this spot on the wedge between William, Lake, and East Clinton Streets. The first school was built in 1862, the second in 1892, and the third in 1913, with an extention added in 1938. Elmira Free Academy moved to Hoffman Street in the early 1960s. Finn Academy exists in the spot today.

South-Side High School at Elmira, N. Y. — 10

By the 1920s a high school was needed on the Southside. Southside High School opened on the corner of Pennsylvania Avenue and South Main Street in 1924. It was one of the first junior-senior high schools in New York. Publisher: Elmira Tobacco Company, Elmira.

A postcard view of Parley Coburn School on Mount Zoar Street, circa 1945. This building was erected in 1930 for grades 1 - 8. Building is still in use. Publisher: Rubin Brothers, Elmira.

Churches

Postcard view of the Park Church on West Church Street, circa 1910. The church was completed in 1873 using the design concepts of the Reverend Thomas K. Beecher in the 1870s. It had a dance floor, a stage, the first public library in Elmira, and a billiard room. Publisher: Paul C. Koeber Co., New York City.

INTERIOR OF GRACE CHURCH ELMIRA, N.Y.

Grace Church on Church Street had its beginning from a split with Trinity Church in 1864. Citing differences in sentiments over Civil War issues, 47 families seceded and formed this church. Publisher: The Metropolitan News Company, Boston, Mass.

Trinity Church at the corner of North Main and West Church Streets, on a snowy day circa 1930. This building still stands. Publisher: unknown.

The First German Evangelical Church on Madison Avenue organized in 1874 on East Church Street. When the congregation outgrew their first building they built this new one in 1899. Many descendants of the original founding families still attend. It is now called the First United Church of Christ. Publisher: Buffalo News Company, Buffalo, NY.

St. Patrick's Church was built in 1874 on West Clinton Street and is still in use. Publisher: Queen City Paper Company, Elmira.

St. Patrick's Catholic Church, Elmira, N. Y. — D-16

The First Baptist Church on West Church Street borders Wisner Park. This is the congregation's third building. It was built in 1892. Publisher: unknown.

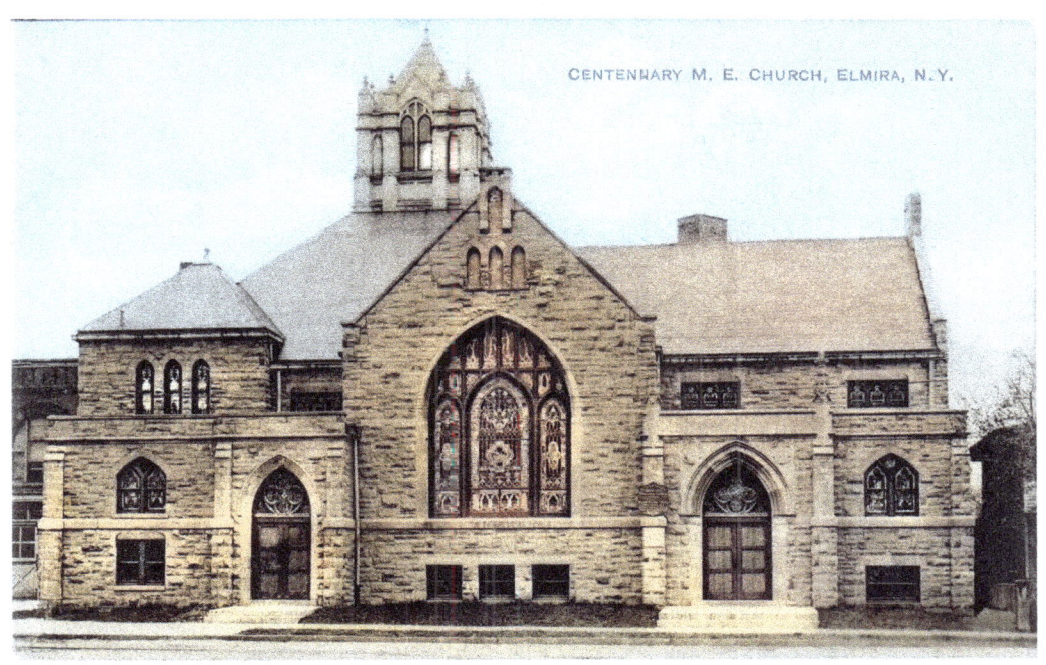

Centenary Methodist Church, built in 1901, on South Main Street was torn down in 2007 to make way for a drug store. Publisher: Baker Brothers, Elmira.

St. Cecilia's church on Lake Street opened in 1904. On the second floor was a school with over 200 students enrolled. The church closed early in the 21st century. The building still exists with a new congregation. Publisher: unknown.

Parks

A lovely view of Wisner Park, circa 1900, with the Langdon home barely visible in the background (behind the trolley). Publisher: C.S. Woolworth, Elmira.

Main Street looking south through Wisner Park. The park is Elmira's town square. William Jennings Bryan spoke here in 1896. Until 1858, Wisner Park was the Baptist cemetery. When Woodlawn Cemetery opened, all the burials were removed. The house on the right in the background is where the Arena is today. Publisher: Valentine & Sons Publishing, New York.

VICTORY ARCH AND MAIN STREET, ELMIRA, N. Y.

The concrete Victory Arch across North Main Street at Wisner Park was built in less than three days notice and was ready in time for the return of Company L from France in April 1919. It did not last very long. This view is looking north. Publisher: Rubin Brothers, Elmira.

Deluxe Big Book of Pictures

View of the Thomas K. Beecher statue in Wisner Park with Park Church in the backgrounds. Beecher was the minister at Park Church from 1854 until his death in 1900. This statue was erected the following year and was flanked by two Sequoia saplings. The trees did not survive in our climate. Publisher: publisher: The Metropolitan News Company, Boston, Mass.

A beautiful day in Wisner Park, circa 1890. View looking northeast with Trinity Church in the background. Publisher: Rubin Brothers, Elmira.

The fountain in Brand Park near the Madison Avenue bridge, circa 1915. Publisher: unknown.

The house on the left was the home of John Brand on Maple Avenue. It was built in 1875. Mr. Brand grew 600 acres of tobacco on the Southside. He donated land for Riverside Park, now known as Brand Park. Today his home is an apartment house and the house on the right is the "Christmas House." Postcard circa 1900. Publisher: Baker Brothers, Elmira.

Maple Avenue looking southeast, circa 1920. Brand Park is on the left, and the John Brand house is on the left in the distance. Publisher: Rubin Brothers, Elmira.

Brand Park, originally called "Riverside Park" or "Elm Tree Park," circa 1900. John Brand donated land from his tobacco plantation for the city park. His home is in the background. Postcard publisher: Paul C. Koeber Co., New York City.

A lovely postcard view of Brand Park from the corner of Maple Avenue looking toward Catherine Street. Catherine Street was named for Catherine Sly - the Sly family being early pioneers on Elmira's Southside. Publisher: Valentine & Sons Publishing, New York & Boston.

RIVERSIDE PARK--FOUNTAIN AND BAND STAND, ELMIRA, N.Y.

The bandstand in Brand Park, circa 1910 with the Brand tobacco warehouse in the background on the left. Publisher: Rubin Brothers, Elmira.

Brand Park pavillion, circa 1910. This pavillion is in approximately the same location as the current one. Brand Park was on land given to the city by John Brand. Brand grew 600 acres of tobacco on the Southside. Publisher: Mac Greevey-Slegt, Elmira.

Wood Path, Elm-Tree Park, Elmira, N.Y.

This postcard is marked "Elm-Tree Park" (today's Brand Park). The wood path went along the river from Madison Avenue bridge to near Esty Street. Publisher: S.F. Iszard Co., Elmira.

Postcard view of the swimming pool in Brand Park, circa 1940. The park had its first swimming pool built in the 1930s with a new one built in 1948. It has been closed since 2005. Publisher: unknown.

Grove Park (the former Hoffman's Grove) became a city park in 1886. Publisher: Paul C. Koeber, New York.

Clark's Glen was a trolley stop in West Elmira just past the city limits. Publisher: The Hugh C. Leighton Co., Portland, ME.

Rorick's Glen

Postcard view of Rorick's Glen bridge over the Chemung River, circa 1907. The walking bridge connected to Rorick's Glen Parkway on the Westside where trolleys ran every quarter hour. Rorick's Glen had something for everybody - a theatre, an amusement park, a restaurant, a dance hall, and plenty of hiking trails. Publisher S. F. Iszard Company, Elmira.

Electric flower beds were all the rage around the turn of the century. They supposedly kept the ground warmer, prevented weeds from growing, and kept out garden pests. This garden was at Rorick's Glen, circa 1915. Publisher: Baker Brothers, Elmira.

The tall contraption in the foreground was a "flying merry-go-round" - you got on and it twirled you around in a big circle over the river. At the other side of the bridge is Rorick's Glen Parkway. Note the big open fields of West Elmira. Publisher: unknown.

A daytime view of Rorick's Glen theater, circa 1915. The theater seated 1200. Publisher: Raphael Tuck & Sons, Holland.

A nighttime view of the Rorick's Glen theater. Stock companies played at Rorick's from 1900 to 1920 and entertained Elmirans with everthing from vaudeville to opera. The theater building burned in 1932. Publisher: Baker Brothers, Elmira.

Eldridge Park

The Eldridge Park Casino was built in 1875. Dr. Eldridge did not allow alcohol or gambling in this building, but it did have a restaurant, an ice cream parlor and wide porches. Photographer: unknown.

A photograph by W. T. Purviance for the Erie Railway, circa 1875. Purviance did a series of photographs called "The Scenery of the Erie Railway" and at some point stopped in Elmira for a visit. Purviance had studios in Philadelphia and Watkins Glen, NY. His advertisement in *Lehigh Valley Railroad Tourist's Guide to Summer Resorts 1875* says he is noted for his photographs of "American Scenery."

Another view of the Casino. It stood just inside the park's main entrance on the left. Publisher: Paul C. Koeber, New York.

A postcard view of young people sitting and contemplating Eldridge Lake, circa 1915. Publisher: Baker Brothers, Elmira.

The Spring House provided thirsty guests with cool sulphur water. Publisher: Baker Brothers, Elmira.

A view of statuary in Eldridge Park, circa 1897. The building on the left is the train station/dance hall. It was torn down in the 1990s when the park was redesigned. Publisher: Valentine & Sons, New York.

Stereograph albumen print by J. H. Whitley, Elmira. *"Dr. Eldridge has men constantly employed to keep his park in order, and had made, we are told, provision in the disposition of his property to have this kept up for all time to come, free to the public."* - J. H. Whitley

Elisha Van Aken took this albumen photo high atop the Casino looking north toward the horse race track, circa 1875. The grand stand in the distance was along McCann's Boulevard. Much of the land to the south of the race track is today a swamp. Around 1880 the Delaware, Lackawanna & Western Railroad extended its rail line through the park and the race track and portion of the park east of Grand Central Avenue was abandoned.

A postcard view of the Eldridge Lake with the Casino in the background, dated 1907. Publisher: Paul C. Koeber Co., New York City.

Elmira photographer C. Tomlinson took this stereograph view "Beauties of Eldridge Park" on a beautiful day around 1880. His studio was on Baldwin Street.

The Chemung River

The Chemung River, probably near Fitch's Bridge, circa 1915. Publisher: Acmegraph Co., Chicago.

A beautiful day on the Chemurg River, circa 1910. Publisher: Buffalo News Company, Buffalo.

The Mountain House on the bottom right was a notorious tavern and stage coach stop between Elmira and Big Flats. It was a wild place in the 1800s. Today this road is Route 352. Postcard image circa 1910. Publisher: unknown.

Looking east down the Chemung River from the Mountain House. Postcard circa 1910. Publisher: Hugh C. Leighton, Portland, ME.

A postcard view of the Chemung River near Rorick's Glen. Publisher: Rubin Brothers, Elmira.

A postcard view of the cottages in the Arcadia area, west of Fitch's Bridge. Publisher: Baker Brothers, Elmira.

Lake Street bridge was modernized in 1905 and replaced in 1961. This photographic view is circa 1920, looking south from the Hulett Building. Publisher: Rubin Brothers, Elmira.

Postcard view of the Main Street bridge, circa 1940. Built in 1920, it lasted until the 1972 flood, and the current bridge opened in 1976. Of interest is the architecture along Water Street. Publisher: Elmira News Co., Elmira.

The dam in the Chemung River at the foot of College Avenue still exists. Publisher: Acmegraph Company, Chicago.

Looking west toward Walnut Street bridge and Mount Zoar, circa 1920. The Walnut Street bridge was swept away in the 1972 flood and was rebuilt a few years later. Postcard publisher: unknown.

Postcard view looking west toward Brand Park from East Hill, circa 1915. Publisher: Jeannette Adams, Elmira.

A view of Elmira looking west from East Hill, circa 1900. The railroad bridge in the foreground still exists. Publisher: Jeannette Adams, Elmira.

Mountain Top Restaurant overlooking the Chemung River near Waverly, New York, circa 1935. The restaurant had a knotty pine interior and was well known for its steak dinners. Building no longer exists. Publisher: Rubin Brothers, Elmira.

The Chemung River looking west from the Main Street bridge, circa 1915. Postcard publisher: unknown.

A postcard view of the Chemung River looking northwest, circa 1915. Note the Hulett Building (the tallest one), the Lake Street bridge, and the backsides of the buildings on East Water Street. Publisher: unknown.

A postcard view of the river from Bohemia Heights, circa 1910. Publisher: Baker Brothers, Elmira.

Deluxe Big Book of Pictures

A postcard view of the water toboggan next to Fitch's Bridge in today's West Elmira. Owned by Mr. and Mrs. John Frantz, whose rule was "Only persons in bathing suits are allowed to take the plunge into the river." Circa 1906. Courtesy of the Barnes family.

Trains and Railroads

The Elmira, Cortland and Northern (later the Lehigh Valley) railroad depot on the northwest corner of East Fifth and Baldwin Streets, circa 1949. This depot was built in 1883. The EC&N was proud of its 4½ hour service from Elmira to Syracuse. Service ended in 1938, and the building was razed in 1950. Today an empty lot marks the spot. Ramsey's bar is visible on the right. Photograph courtesy of Robert Rockwell.

Postcard view of the first Delaware, Lackawanna & Western railroad station at the foot of Benjamin Street on Elmira's Eastside, circa 1890. Publisher: unknown.

Postcard view of the second Delaware, Lackawanna & Western railroad station at the foot of Benjamin Street on Elmira's Eastside, circa 1920. The Lackawanna tracks were raised in Elmira in 1933. This station was built around 1910 and lasted until 1959, when the Lackawanna Railroad merged with the Erie Railroad. All that is left today is the impressive terrazzo floor. Publisher: Rubin Brothers, Elmira.

The Delaware, Lackawanna, & Western bridge over Newtown Creek near East Water Street. The bridge still exists and is awaiting transformation to become part of a trail system. Postcard view circa 1910. Publisher: unknown.

The Union Depot (later Erie, and then Erie-Lackawanna depot) opened in 1865. In its heyday, this depot was shared by New York & Erie Railroad, and the Northern Central division of the Pennsylvania Railroad. The Erie tracks were raised in Elmira in 1934. The depot closed in 1970 but the building still exists. Publisher: unknown.

Elmira College

Attributed to J. E. Larkin, this albumen stereograph print is of Cowles Hall at the "Elmira Female College," (today's Elmira College) circa 1865. Larkin was well known for his photographs of the Elmira Prison Camp. This building is still used.

Postcard view of Hamilton Hall on the campus of Elmira College is an example of English Collegiate Gothic architecture. It was built in 1927 and was originally the college's library, later the art department. Currently it houses the Office of Admissions, Financial Aid, Alumni Relations, Development, and Parent Relations. Publisher: Rubin Brothers, Elmira.

Fassett Commons - dining hall at Elmira College was built in 1916. View looking northeast toward Washington Avenue. Building still exists but it is not the dining hall any longer. Publisher: Rubin Brothers, Elmira.

A postcard view of Sarah Tompkins Hall on the Elmira College campus. This building is still used. Publisher: Rubin Brothers, Elmira.

The Carnegie Science Building on the Elmira College campus built in 1911 still exists. Publisher: Rubin Brothers, Elmira.

Elmira College's first Alumnae Hall (the sophomore dormitory) on West Washington Avenue. This building was built in 1916 and razed in the 1960s. A new Alumni Hall was built along North Main Street. Publisher: Rubin Brothers, Elmira.

Landscapes

A beautiful scene along a creek or Chemung River channel, circa 1900. Photographer: unknown.

A happy group next to Fitch's Bridge, circa 1915. Photograph courtesy of the Barnes family.

Farmers trying out the "Union Leader" on their crops. Postcard circa 1917. Field Force manufactured power spraying machines and pumps in Elmira Heights. Postcard publisher: unknown.

7681—View of Chemung River, Elmira, N.Y.

A postcard view of the bend of the Chemung River looking north, near the foot of Esty Street. Circa 1890. Publisher: Souvenir Post Card, Company, NY.

A postcard view from Rorick's Glen looking east. Publisher: Baker Brothers, Elmira, NY.

A postcard view on Harris Hill - the "Soaring Capital of the World." Regional and national soaring meets have been held here since the 1930s. Publisher: Elmira News Company, Elmira.

The original Sullivan's Monument, dedicated to General John Sullivan on his centennial anniversary in 1879. It began crumbling and finally collapsed in 1911 - hopefully not the day this young woman was sitting so precariously. Photograph courtesy of the Barnes family.

Above is the new Sullivan's Monument dedicated in 1912 and still standing. Publisher: Rubin Brothers, Elmira.

Arnot Mill, or Tuttle Mill across Newtown Creek at East Water Street, circa 1900. Originally built by Stephen Tuttle and Guy Maxwell, the mill was one of the first flour mills in central New York. Publisher: Rubin Brothers, Elmira.

The postcard's title is wrong - this is actually looking toward Wellsburg from Sullivan's Monument. Publisher: Rubin Brothers, Elmira.

Just a pretty scene in the Chemung Valley. Publisher: The Rotograph Co., NY City.

Mark Twain

"Quarry Farm," Mark Twain's Summer Home, Elmira, N. Y. — 19

This is Quarry Farm on East Hill. It was Mark Twain's (Samuel Clemens') beloved summer home during the 1870s and 80s. He wrote much of his important work in Elmira. Mark is buried nearby with his family in Elmira's Woodlawn Cemetery. Postcard publisher: Elmira Tobacco Company.

Mark Twain, also known as Samuel Clemens, and his family spent many summers at Quarry Farm, east of Elmira. Publisher: Rubin Brothers, Elmira.

Side view of Quarry Farm. Publisher: Rubin Brothers, Elmira.

Mark Twain worked in this little study high above Elmira at Quarry Farm. His study was given to Elmira College in 1952 and is a popular tourist destination. Publisher: Elmira News Company.

Another postcard view of Mark Twain's study. Publisher: Rubin Brothers. Elmira.

An interior view of Mark Twain's study. The study now stands along Park Place on the Elmira College campus. Publisher: Rubin Brothers. Elmira.

Mark Twain's grave in Woodlawn Cemetery in Elmira. It is a popular tourist destination. Publisher: Queen City Paper Company, Elmira.

Grave of Mark Twain at Woodlawn Cemetery, Elmira, N. Y. — D-

Deluxe Big Book of Pictures

So long from Elmira, New York. Wish you were here! Publisher: Rubin Brothers, Elmira.

Bibiliography

Biographical Record of Chemung County, New York. New York and Chicago: The S. J. Clarke Publishing Company, 1902.

History of Tioga, Chemung, Tompkins, and Schuyler Counties, New York with Biographical Sketches of some of its prominent men and pioneers. Philadelphia: Everts & Ensign, 1879.

Taylor, Eva. *A Short History of Elmira*. Elmira, New York: Steele Memorial Library, 1937.

Towner, Ausburn. *Our County and Its People, A History of the Chemung Valley and County of Chemung from the closing years of the eighteenth century*. : D. Mason & Co., 1892.

More books from New York History Review

A Short and Sweet History of the Chemung Valley
The Park Church Souvenir Cookbook of 1906
The Great Inter-State Fair
Zim's Foolish History of Elmira
Zim's Foolish History of Horseheads
Frederick Douglass' Speech at Elmira
In Their Honor
In Dairyland
The True Stories series
A Brief History of Chemung County
Cartoons and Caricatures
Our Own Book
The Elmira Prison Camp